Wo

l

Eight Dates

Essential Conversations for a Lifetime of Love

(A Guide to John Gottman Ph.D. et al.,'s Book)

By

Genius Minds

INTRODUCTION

We all want to have a happy and lasting relationship or marriage. However, that can be very hard if we don't have certain important conversations with our partners. Your partner doesn't have to be exactly like you for your relationships to work. This book will help you navigate the different important topics you need to have with your partner for your relationship to grow and be happy. It also emphasizes on the importance of dates, listening to your partner and figuring things out together. It can be hard to maintain relationships with all the curveballs life throws at us but with this book it might just be a tad easier.

THE CONVERSATIONS THAT MATTER

OBJECTIVES
1. Asking open-ended questions.
2. Understanding the science of love.
3. Understanding what determines a happy couple.

A true love story isn't a fairytale; it requires vulnerability and effort. More than half of marriages in the United States reportedly end in divorce. The divorce rate increases to 65% with second marriages and to 75% with third marriages. Even though the odds are poor, there is still hope. It's not about luck; it's up to you. The Gottman Love Lab has been researching how to succeed in love for 40 years and they now understand what a couple can do to increase their chances. They collected synchronized physiological, self-report, and observational data from couples in their Seattle lab, and used sophisticated mathematical techniques to analyze the data. After observing thousands of couples, they now know the areas most couples struggle with. They can also guide you through the eight important discussions that will give you the best opportunity of getting your own happily ever after. Modest words, actions, and small gestures build successful long-term relationships. Every single day that you are together with your partner, a lifetime of love is created. Love does not require perfection; it requires practice. More than a feeling, love is an action. The key to developing a love that endures is straightforward; prioritize spending time together and never stop being interested in your partner. In other words, keep asking questions but make sure it's the right questions. Ask open-ended questions not questions that require a yes-or-no answer. Open-ended questions allow the other person to really talk about their opinions and experiences. This will allow you to understand your partner's beliefs, actions, and personality. They can help you fall in love, decide to get married, or stay in love with the person you've decided to spend the rest of your life with. Trust and commitment, conflict, sex, money, family, fun and adventure, growth and spirituality, and dreams are the eight issues that have the biggest impact on relationships. These issues have been divided into eight dates for you to attend. According to research, the best relationships are based on mutual respect, empathy, and a deep understanding of one another. Having a great relationship doesn't mean there's no conflict or problems. Every relationship faces conflict. Every day, life presents us with its fair share of pressures and crises, and how you deal with them as a team will ultimately determine whether you succeed or fail. Happily ever after simply means both partners are acknowledged, cherished, and accepted for who they are and who they are changing into. Each year you spend together, the goal is to be able to love your partner more.

THE SCIENCE OF LOVE

John and his colleague Robert Levenson had a lab at the University of Washington. It was an innovative research facility devoted to learning the truth about marriage and divorce. Their research questions include: Can we predict who will get divorced and who will stay married, happily or unhappily? And what actually makes relationships work well? 130 newlywed couples checked into the apartment, which became known as "The Love Lab" forever, for one of the lab's largest studies so they could be observed 24 hours a day while they went about their daily lives as they normally would if they were at home. Everything was normal except for the three cameras in the apartment walls that watched their every move and the specially designed monitors worn by each participant, which monitored their electrocardiogram physiology. Each couple's vital signs were tracked, their body language was analyzed, and each couple's facial expressions were coded by John and his team of experts. They also conducted two-hour oral history interviews with couples as an important part of their laboratory research. Researchers observed the tone of voice, words, gestures, and positive and negative emotions of each participant during these interviews. Last but not least, John also invited each couple to talk about a current argument they were having. It was a long and thorough research. At the end, John was able to predict who would get married and who would finally get divorced with an accuracy of 94%.

POSITIVE OR NEGATIVE

After a decade of analyzing the data from the Love Lab, John discovered that one set of variables determined if a marriage would succeed or fail: During the interview, were the couples being positive or negative? Either they focused on the positive moments they shared while downplaying the negative ones, or they focused on the negative moments while downplaying the positive ones. Couples that are most likely to have happy marriages exhibit the following traits and features listed below when they discuss their relationship:

1. Fondness, affection, admiration: The couple compliments each other and shows positive affections like warmth, humor, and tenderness both verbally and nonverbally.
2. We-ness versus separateness: The couple highlights their excellent communication skills, their shared unity and togetherness. Instead of using a lot of "I," "me," or "mine," they use terms like "we," "us," or "our." They don't think of themselves as separate.

3. Glorifying the struggle: In a relationship, two people create a complete life together, one that is full of values, goals, and meaning. The couple shows pride in overcoming hardship by "glorifying the struggle" talking about how hard that time was. They place more emphasis on their dedication to their partner instead of whether they should truly be with them. They are proud of their relationship and not ashamed of it. They talk about their beliefs, aspirations, and way of life. They create intentional traditions in their relationship to build emotional ties. These are called connection rituals. Dates are an example.

If a couple starts the interview by being critical of one another, it shows that the negative switch is on and this means the relationship will get worse over time. Divorce is more likely if the couple shows dissatisfaction or is resentful of their union. However, it is important to know that every relationship has problems. The positive switch focuses on how couples interpret their negative experiences and their partner's personality, and if they consistently highlight the good and minimize the bad in their brains. A relationship will be quickly destroyed by an overall perception of negativity. Every successful marriage and relationship is built on a strong and close friendship between the partners. A happy relationship is not a relationship without conflict. The only difference between happy and unhappy couples is that happy couples find a way to fix their relationship more quickly and easily, which allows them to rediscover the joy of being together.

THE BIGGER PICTURE

The nature of our closest relationships affects our physical health and lifespan. Close relationships that are satisfying improves the mental health of each partner on numerous levels. Long-term relationships and successful marriages have been shown to reduce suicidal thoughts and behaviors as well as addictions and depression. Numerous studies have also shown that while good relationships can improve children's academic achievement, peer relationships, and emotional intelligence, long-term unhappy relationships can harm children's cognitive and emotional health. Being in a committed relationship requires work. We all want to love and be loved. Everybody wants to develop their relationships and this means stepping out of your comfort zone. Your relationship will improve if you're prepared to be open-minded about your spouse and honest about who you truly are.

LESSONS
1. Love is not just a feeling; it is an action.
2. Love requires practice not perfection.

3. Trust and commitment, conflict, sex, money, family, fun and adventure, growth and spirituality, and dreams are the eight issues that have the biggest impact on relationships.
4. Conflict is a part of every relationship.
5. Dates are an example of connection rituals.
6. The best relationships are based on mutual respect, empathy, and a deep understanding of one another.
7. Our relationships affect our physical well-being and lifespan.
8. How a couple talks about their partner and relationship is one way to determine if the relationship would succeed or fail.

QUESTIONS
1. What do you think is the biggest issue in your relationship?

_____
_____
_____
_____
_____
_____
_____
_____
_____
_____
_____
_____
_____

2. What are the benefits of asking open-ended questions?

_____
_____
_____
_____
_____
_____
_____
_____
_____
_____
_____
_____
_____

3. What does happily ever after mean to you?

_____
_____
_____
_____
_____
_____
_____
_____
_____
_____
_____
_____

4. How has your relationship affected you recently?

_____
_____
_____
_____
_____
_____
_____
_____
_____
_____
_____

5. How have you stepped out of your comfort zone in your relationship?

_____
_____
_____
_____
_____
_____
_____
_____
_____
_____

6. Why did you choose your current partner?

7. What are the benefits of a successful relationship?

8. What are the problems in your current relationship?

_____
_____
_____
_____
_____

9. How did your parent's relationship affect you as a child?

_____
_____
_____
_____
_____
_____
_____
_____
_____
_____
_____

10. What's the difference between the positive and negative switch?

_____
_____
_____
_____
_____
_____
_____
_____
_____
_____
_____
_____
_____
_____

YOUR DATE NIGHT

OBJECTIVES
1. Making your relationship a priority.
2. Defining a date.
3. Overcoming the obstacles of date night.

Little kind gestures are what make the difference in relationships. These little gestures are the foundation of your relationship so you should cherish them. This book will walk you through eight different dates that will improve your relationship. Making a special date once a week a priority can help you achieve your relationship's goals. Date nights for many busy couples often turn into haphazard, freakish occurrences, especially once they have kids. However, date nights shouldn't be accidental events that only occur when opportunity, finances, and laundry all synchronize in some ideal and magical way. Date nights make relationships. A date is a time that the two of you have set aside when you both put everything else aside and spend a specific amount of time actually paying attention to each other. A date is a unique time reserved for you and your partner to get to know one another. Turn off or leave your electronics at home, and check them only after the date is ended. Consider every one of these eight dates to be your first. Plan them, aim to enjoy them and be ecstatic about them.

DATE NIGHT OBSTACLES
1. Time: Finding time for a date can seem impossible when life is already so hectic. However, a date night is more than just a requirement; it's a commitment to your partnership and your dreams of a successful marriage. Make date night a "no matter what" occasion unless someone needs to be sent to the emergency room. Date nights have to be special occasions to respect your union.
2. Money: Dates don't have to cost a lot of money. There are plenty of inexpensive methods to spend time with your loved one. It could be a picnic, a walk etc.
3. Childcare: For couples who want to go on date nights but have young children at home, childcare is sometimes the stumbling block. It doesn't have to be expensive. You can switch with friends to watch each other's children. If that isn't possible, ask a close friend or family member for help. Ask your friends for referrals or look around your community for affordable babysitters. Children are quite resilient and by showing your dedication to your relationship with your spouse, you are nourishing your children by

making sure that they will be brought up by parents in a happy and stable relationship. Children benefit from a marriage's love. You want children to witness how you maintain a loving marriage since they are always modeling you.

A FEW GUIDELINES

1. Read a little: Read each chapter before the date. Each chapter starts with an explanation of why a particular subject is important to your relationship and what you need to know to make it part of your happy relationship.
2. Talk a lot: Bring the list of open-ended questions for that specific date topic with you. These will act as your conversation guide.
3. Drink little or not at all: On date night, keep your drug and alcohol intake to a minimum. Many couples find that drinking together increases their likelihood of fighting. On each date, try to limit your alcohol consumption to no more than one wine glass. You want to be fully present when having conversations. Make sure the restaurants where you go on dates are places where you can speak to each other freely and plainly hear each other if you want to spend most of your time there.
4. Keep a sense of humor: Find the funny moments. During hard times, try to find joy. Remember the reasons you fell in love with each other, and most importantly, never stop laughing.

LESSONS

1. Little kind gestures and actions are the foundation of a relationship.
2. Date nights should be a priority and not last-minute rushes.
3. A date is a unique time reserved for you and your partner to get to know one another.
4. Dates don't have to be expensive; they can be anything you can you partner likes.

QUESTIONS

1. How often do you and your partner have date nights?

_____
_____
_____
_____
_____
_____
_____
_____

_____
_____
_____
_____

2. What are the obstacles stopping you from having regular date nights?

_____
_____
_____
_____
_____
_____
_____
_____
_____
_____
_____

3. What do you and your partner like to do on your date nights?

_____
_____
_____
_____
_____
_____
_____
_____
_____
_____
_____

4. What are the little actions your partner does in your relationship that are important to you?

_____
_____
_____
_____

_____
_____
_____
_____
_____
_____
_____
_____
_____

5. How do children benefit from a happy relationship or marriage?

_____
_____
_____
_____
_____
_____
_____
_____
_____
_____
_____
_____
_____
_____
_____
_____
_____
_____
_____
_____
_____
_____
_____
_____
_____
_____

THE ART OF LISTENING

Asking open-ended questions during your dates is important but listening is also very important. However, it is important to listen without judgement or rebuttals. Listening is an action and it requires commitment. It is important that you get out of your own head and listen to your partner.

1. Be attentive: Turn off your gadgets and pay attention to whatever they are saying. It is important that you maintain eye contact and pay attention to what your partner is saying.

2. Be present: Listening is more than just keeping quiet when the other person is talking. When you are actively listening, don't assume you know what your partner will say next. You also don't plan your response or think about it as your partner is speaking. Just listen.

3. Ask questions: Ask questions if you don't understand something. Open-ended questions open the heart. Do not hesitate to ask clarifying questions like "Can you tell me more about that?" Also remember that this is a conversation not an interrogation.

4. Tune in: Your responsibility as a listener is to pay attention to your partner's emotions. Make sure you don't disregard or try to fix your partner's feelings.

5. Avoid judgment: Don't criticize or offer advice until your partner asks for it. Every time you talk to your partner, you want to show respect, understanding and empathy. Remember, the goal is not to show that you are correct or that your partner is mistaken. The goal is to understand the similarities and differences between you.

Although it's not always easy for us, listening is important for intimate conversations. You can direct your dates and your relationship by asking each other questions as you listen to one another. They'll eventually come naturally. Here are some examples of questions you can use to understand your partner; What emotions do you have? How can I help? What's the worst that can happen in this situation? What's your perfect dream for the situation? If you do not understand each other, take a big breath. These dates aren't for working out differences.

DATE 1: LEAN ON ME: TRUST & COMMITMENT

OBJECTIVES
1. Defining commitment.
2. Understanding the importance of commitment.
3. Repairing broken trust.

CHOOSING COMMITMENT

Commitment is a decision we make every day even when we are exhausted, overworked, and under stress. We show our loyalty when we make our relationship a priority. The Love Lab discovered that it is the little, kind things we do that have the biggest impact on our relationships and help to create that safe, trusting environment. What does true commitment mean? It means that we reject potential relationships with others as we are emotionally and sexually devoted to our partners. Outside of marriage, we uphold boundaries in our relationships. The late Dr. Shirley Glass discovered in her book Not Just Friends that when people, especially those who are dissatisfied in their relationships, start confiding in another person about their relationship, they are opening up a window to this outside person. They also build a wall in their relationship when they hide this new platonic or emotional relationship from their partners. If you want to have long-term trust, dedication, and loyalty, there can't be walls between you. Committing to someone can be terrifying; there is no security net. You can't tell anyone when things are not going smoothly you must resolve issues with our partner directly. It's all or nothing with this person. It's a risky choice but it's necessary. When you choose commitment, you must accept your partner's shortcomings. This means never threatening to leave, even if there are times you want to. It also means seeing your partner's suffering as your own. True commitment is constantly making the decision to be in a relationship and making it work. Every betrayal starts with Negative Comps. This is when people start comparing their partners with other people. They wish their partners had certain things or behaviors of someone else. Instead of discussing our concerns with our partner, we fantasize about being in a different relationship with someone else and how we might get what is missing from our current connection with them.

DISCOVERING YOUR OWN WONDERLAND

There will be a time in your relationship when things become hard and in that dark moment, you might wonder if you picked the right partner. In committed relationships, people don't have one foot out the door. When things in their relationship aren't going well, they talk to their partner and not someone else. It can be frightening to commit to a relationship since it requires vulnerability. When we start a new relationship, we only show our good side. However, as the relationship grows, each person becomes more open, honest, and vulnerable. No matter how put together we may seem, none of us has it completely together. The more open-minded we are, the more likely it is that our partner will accept us for who we are rather than the idealized version of us they had in their head in the beginning. Relationships require trust which creates vulnerability. Also, trust builds over time and through conversations. Trust is the foundation of any relationship. When we show our partner that we are there for them and they reciprocate, we develop trust. There are different ways people betray trust in a relationship, but these are the most typical: being late, not prioritizing their relationship with their partner, failing to keep promises, keeping secrets, lying, humiliating your partner in front of others or in private, being abusive physically.

WHEN TRUST HAS BEEN BROKEN

There are steps you can take to fix broken trust; you cannot skip any of these procedures;

1. Set a time and place for your conversation.
2. Without assigning blame or offering criticism, each person talks about how they felt during the incident or breach of trust.
3. The receiving partner listens without criticism.
4. Without condemning or criticizing their partner, each person talks about their view on what happened while the other person only listens and makes an effort to empathize. When someone is speaking, the listener shouldn't interrupt with their own opinion.
5. Explain and analyze any emotions that were triggered by the situation.
6. Each partner evaluates how they contributed to the situation and accepts responsibility.
7. Both parties express regret and accept the other's apology.
8. Together, you come up with a strategy to stop the incident from happening again.

LESSONS

1. commitment means that we reject potential relationships with others as we are fully devoted to our partners.
2. Commitment can be scary but it is necessary for your relationship to grow.
3. Negative Comps is when you start comparing your partner with other people.

4. It is important that we become more honest, open and vulnerable as our relationship grows.
5. Trust is the foundation of relationships and it build over time through conversations.
6. When trying to fix trust in your relationship, it is important that you listen without criticism.

QUESTIONS

1. Why is Trust mad commitment important in relationships?

_____
_____
_____
_____
_____
_____
_____
_____
_____
_____
_____
_____

2. What does commitment mean to you?

_____
_____
_____
_____
_____
_____
_____
_____
_____
_____
_____
_____

3. How has your partner shown you their commitment to you?

_____
_____

_____
_____
_____
_____
_____
_____
_____
_____
_____
_____

4. How has your partner broken your trust in the past?

_____
_____
_____
_____
_____
_____
_____
_____
_____
_____
_____

5. What does trust look like in your relationship?

_____
_____
_____
_____
_____
_____
_____
_____
_____
_____
_____

6. When have you felt like you couldn't trust your partner?

_____

_____

_____

_____

_____

_____

_____

_____

_____

_____

_____

7. What areas do you think you and your partner need to work on to build trust in your relationship?

_____

_____

_____

_____

_____

_____

_____

_____

_____

_____

_____

8. Who do you tend to compare your partner to and why?

_____

_____

_____

_____

_____

_____

_____

_____

9. How can you fix broken trust?

_____
_____
_____
_____
_____
_____
_____
_____
_____
_____
_____
_____
_____
_____
_____

10. What have you done to ensure that you don't break your partner's trust?

_____
_____
_____
_____
_____
_____
_____
_____
_____
_____
_____
_____
_____
_____
_____
_____

DATE 2: AGREE TO DISAGREE: ADDRESSING CONFLICT

OBJECTIVES
1. Managing conflict.
2. Differentiating solvable and perpetual problems.
3. Learning how to fix your issues.

Conflict is part of life. One of the biggest illusions about marriage is that if you never argue or talk about uncomfortable or tough subjects, your marriage is good. When you are married, you're more than just two people who came together.

MANAGING CONFLICT
The best time to talk about managing conflict is not during an argument. It is important to understand that conflict is normal and has a purpose. So what is the purpose of conflict? Many people believe that conflict is unhealthy but it is necessary as we face issues when trying to love one another. Over time, resolving disagreement makes it easier for us to love and understand each other more deeply and to reaffirm our commitment to the relationship. According to research, most interpersonal conflict cannot be resolved. Each relationship has its own set of issues because every individual is different and unique, there will always be issues will always arise no matter who the other partner is. Many of our issues follow us around, resurfacing in every relationship until we eventually learn to identify and effectively handle them. Most problems are either perpetual or solvable problems. Solvable problems are situational problems. Examples are problems about cleaning, who picks up the kids, where to go on vacation etc. These are problems that can be solved. However, this does not always mean easy. Solving these issues requires effort and action. Perpetual problems are issues that are caused by basic differences in your personalities or lifestyle. These are the issues that you keep coming back to. You shouldn't try to fix these issues by changing because you can't. Accepting your partner as they are is important when handling conflict. You accept one another when you accept the things you cannot change. It is important that you honor and appreciate each other's differences.

A WORD ABOUT GRIDLOCK
Gridlock is the sense of being trapped and going nowhere; no one likes it. This happens if you find yourself in a never-ending argument over a certain issue. If you find yourself having the same conversations with no solution, your perpetual problem has become gridlocked. This often leads to you and your partner feeling frustrated. Conflict can help you become closer with your partner if you choose

to see it as a way to get to know your partner better. With each conflict, you can build a stronger relationship if you sincerely try to understand your partner's point of view. Try asking yourself or even your partner what he or she needs when they show anger. When we truly love someone, we love all of them, and accept them as they are.

FIGHT FAIR AND REPAIR

All relationships will eventually have issues. Research shows that happy couples resolve their differences amicably. They try to understand their partner, listen to their perspective, and work together to create a solution that benefits both parties. Of course, this is easier said than done. In the moment, we tend to say and do things that hurt our partners. However, master couples are skilled in reducing the harm that can be done by words spoken in anger. Processing a fight involves talking about what happened without starting the fight again. The goal here is not to prove that you're right and they're wrong; it's to understand what reality looks like to the other person.

These are steps you can take when trying to fix issues in your relationship;

1. Each person takes a turn discussing how they felt during the argument.
2. Each person talks about their perspective on the situation. It is possible for both of you to have 2 different perspectives so don't argue and say your partner's view is wrong. Tell your partner that you can see some things from their perspective. Talk about your needs and feelings exclusively. Use "I" statements when doing that. Don't tell your partner what they did or didn't do. Avoid accusing your partner as much as you can.
3. Triggers: These are emotional scars and vulnerabilities from before the past, that is, before the start of the relationship. When you are feeling triggered, try going back in time to a time in your past or your childhood when you had a similar set of emotions. Triggers persist; they don't go away. If you are the one who gets triggered, tell your partner why certain things are a trigger for you so they can understand. If your partner is talking about their triggers and how it affects them, listen, show empathy and understanding.
4. Accept responsibility and acknowledge your part in the issue. Avoid placing blame in this situation. Accepting responsibility helps with solving the issue; it is very effective.
5. Talk about how you two could do and look at things differently in the future to avoid escalating the problem.

LESSONS

1. The problems we face in relationships are either solvable problems or perpetual problems.
2. Triggers are emotional scars and vulnerabilities from the past.
3. Conflict is a way to get to know your partner better; it is easier to solve them when you see it this way.
4. Gridlock is the sense of being trapped and going nowhere.
5. Don't avoid conflict; it is natural and necessary.
6. It is important to know when a problem is solvable and when it's not. Not all conflict can or needs to be resolved.
7. Accepting responsibility is very important when trying to fix the issues in your relationship. Don't put all the blame on your partner.
8. Although conflicts can be beneficial to a relationship, it can also end it if it is not handled properly.

QUESTIONS

1. What is the most recent conflict you've had in your relationship?

_____
_____
_____
_____
_____
_____
_____
_____
_____
_____
_____
_____

2. What's the difference between solvable and perpetual problems?

_____
_____
_____
_____
_____
_____
_____

_____
_____
_____
_____

3. What triggers do you have during conflict and why?

_____
_____
_____
_____
_____
_____
_____
_____
_____
_____
_____

4. What are the differences between you and your partner?

_____
_____
_____
_____
_____
_____
_____
_____
_____
_____
_____
_____

5. What differences can't you accept in a partner?

_____
_____
_____
_____
_____

_____
_____
_____
_____
_____
_____
_____

6. How was conflict resolved in your family?

_____
_____
_____
_____
_____
_____
_____
_____
_____
_____

7. How do you resolve conflict with your partner?

_____
_____
_____
_____
_____
_____
_____
_____
_____
_____

8. What are the effects of avoiding conflict?

_____
_____

_____
_____
_____
_____
_____
_____
_____
_____
_____
_____
_____

9. What is a perpetual problem you currently have in your relationship?

_____
_____
_____
_____
_____
_____
_____
_____
_____
_____
_____

10. How has the conflicts in your relationship helped you understand your partner?

_____
_____
_____
_____
_____
_____
_____
_____
_____
_____
_____

DATE 3: LET'S GET IT ON: SEX & INTIMACY

OBJECTIVES
1. Understanding the importance of intimacy in a relationship.
2. Initiating sex.
3. Accepting the no.

Talking about sex doesn't have to be awkward, uncomfortable, or serious. Be open-minded and lighthearted when having this discussion and date. It is less stressful and serious when people joke about having sex. It is an effective way to start the conversation.

FINDING YOUR NORMAL
Everyone is curious about other relationships and tends to compare them to theirs. How much sex do they have? How much intimacy is "normal" in a committed relationship? Whatever works for you and your spouse is normal. Thinking that sex is or should be incredibly romantic, with lit candles, soothing music, and hours of lovemaking is a myth. It is not always like this; some couples might do this often and others might have more quickies. There could be role-playing, sex toys etc. Normal can change as your relationship grows depending on what you and your partner find comfortable. Don't ever think you'll have sex everyday at the beginning of a relationship or marriage; you are setting yourself up to fail. This is because life can happen and make it hard to even think about sex. However, there are ways to both strengthen and weaken your connection that don't include being in bed. We all want our relationship to be passionate and connected. Stop making sex the last thing on a very long to-do list. There are practical techniques to guarantee you enjoy a fantastic sexual life and they include; Say "I love you" to your partners every day and mean it, buy surprise romantic gifts, compliment your partner frequently, have romantic vacations, kiss one another passionately for no reason at all, show affection publicly, make sex a priority and talk to one another about sex comfortably etc.

SEX AFTER PARENTHOOD
According to a UCLA Sloane Center for Everyday Life of Families study on dual-career couples, families with young children tend to spend very little time together. It is even worse for families with two working parents. They noticed that most of the conversations the couples had during their limited interactions were about errands. Because of this, a lot of couples eventually stop spending romantic time together and drift apart. The fun stops for them. They stop doing

all the things that helped them maintain desire and a vibrant love life. Instead, their days are consumed by a never-ending list of errands, and life becomes dull. This shouldn't become the norm. It is important that children see a loving relationship between their parents. They are nurtured by this and it gives them something to model.

TALKING ABOUT SEX

According to research, relationships with open communication about sex result in more sex and higher orgasms for the women. Talking about sexual benefits relationships but it can be hard. Only a small percentage of couples are able to discuss sex honestly and openly. However, you can learn and become more comfortable over time. It is important to focus on what you enjoy and what makes you feel good. It's also important to talk about sex outside of the bedroom. It won't work out well for either of you to interrupt the action to offer constructive comments.

INITIATING SEX

According to research, almost 70% of adults ask for sex in indirect ways. Most individuals will touch, cuddle, or kiss to show their desire to make love. It is a "face-saving" method. It's a chance to try things out without getting rejected. Nobody enjoys being rejected. However, as the relationship grows, requests for sex become more direct. This is good because it reduces the likelihood of miscommunication and hurt feelings.

When it comes to asking for sex, men and women generally different;

1. Thinking about sex: Men think about sex more than women.
2. Frequency: Men ideally want to have sex four to five times per week, while women want to have it one to two times weekly.
3. Fantasies: While women tend to have more romantic fantasies, men tend to have more explicit sexual fantasies.
4. Masturbation: Males masturbate more during their teenage years than girls do, and it tend to remain the same even as they grow older.
5. Prerequisites for sex: Women need to feel emotionally connected in order to have sex, and men like to have sex to feel emotionally connected.

ACCEPTING THE NO

Don't get upset if your spouse doesn't want to have sex. Research shows that neither of you will be in the mood 25% of the time that your partner is. The success of your relationship depends on how you handle hearing "no". Even if sex is not an option, find other ways to show affection and be with your partner.

Couples that are adept at accepting no actually have more sex than those where one spouse becomes irritated when the other isn't feeling it. Couples who have mastered accepting the no actually have more sex than those who get offended. It is important not to punish your partner for saying no. Research shows it is harder for men to hear "no," because a man's perception of his manhood depends on feeling wanted sexually. Your sex life will suffer if there isn't any physical affection, flirting, or other intimate connections. Your sex life will suffer if there is no emotional connection or conflict. Monitoring your partner's private life will enhance your sex life.

KEEPING IT PASSIONATE

Kissing is the easiest way to maintain the passion in your relationship. When you kiss passionately, you set off a biological cascade of hormones and neurotransmitters that release dopamine and enhance oxytocin, both of which make you feel wonderful. If you really mean it when you kiss, your blood vessels will widen, your brain will receive additional oxygen, your pupils will dilate, and your cheeks will flush. A nice kiss physically lights up the brain, because kissing stimulates five of the twelve cranial nerves. The world's largest research on love discovered that one universal key to fantastic sex lives was passionate kissing. Verbally expressing your love for, affection for, and gratitude for the other person is another way to maintain passion. Tell your partner the positive things you have about them in your mind. Take time to appreciate their efforts, their beauty, their knowledge, their work, their abilities, their sense of humor, and anything else you like and love about them. Create your own rituals for connecting, give yourself time to date each other and get to know each other on a daily basis. Making love to each other is something you do with your minds and your hearts, not just your body. With time, these kinds of romantic traditions and love acts will increase your attraction for one another.

LESSONS
1. Normal in sex is whatever works for your relationship; don't compare with others.
2. If your partner isn't in the mood to have sex be accepting, loving, and caring. It is important that you don't get angry.
3. Making love isn't just about the body; it also involves the heart and mind.
4. Creating connection rituals increases your attraction for your partner.
5. It is important that you tell your partner the positive thoughts you have about them; it can help build connection.
6. Talking about sex doesn't have to be serious; it can be fun too.

7. Women need to feel emotionally connected in order to have sex while men like to have sex to feel emotionally connected.
8. Kissing releases dopamine and enhances oxytocin.

QUESTIONS
1. How does talking about sex make you feel?

_____
_____
_____
_____
_____
_____
_____
_____
_____
_____
_____
_____
_____

2. What kind of relationship would you say your parents had?

_____
_____
_____
_____
_____
_____
_____
_____
_____
_____
_____
_____

3. How do you ask your partner for sex?

_____
_____
_____
_____
_____

_____
_____
_____
_____
_____
_____
_____
_____

4. What's the typical reaction in your relationship when one of you is not in the mood for sex?

_____
_____
_____
_____
_____
_____
_____
_____
_____
_____
_____

5. What are the things affecting your sex life in your relationship and how can you overcome them?

_____
_____
_____
_____
_____
_____
_____
_____
_____
_____
_____
_____
_____

6. What's the difference between your sex life with your partner when the relationship started and now?

_____

_____

_____

_____

_____

_____

_____

_____

_____

_____

_____

7. What sexual fantasy would you like to try with your partner?

_____

_____

_____

_____

_____

_____

_____

_____

_____

_____

_____

_____

_____

_____

_____

_____

_____

_____

_____

_____

8. What would you like to change about your sex life?

_____
_____
_____
_____
_____
_____
_____
_____
_____
_____
_____
_____

9. What connection rituals do you and your partner do often?

_____
_____
_____
_____
_____
_____
_____
_____
_____
_____
_____
_____

10. What positive thoughts do you have about your partner in your mind?

_____
_____
_____
_____
_____
_____
_____
_____
_____
_____
_____

DATE 4: THE COST OF LOVE: WORK & MONEY

OBJECTIVES
1. Understanding your partner's relationship with money.
2. Understanding how money affects your relationship.
3. Understanding the term "having enough money".

Money is part of the top five causes of marital conflict. According to research, disagreements over money are the single best predictor of divorce among all other marital conflicts. Most couples' disagreements about money tend to fall into one of three categories: different views on financial inequality, different views on what it means to be financially stable and different views on the nature of their disagreements about money. The most important thing is how a couple handles their money conflicts. Couples should try not to compare one another to the Spender and the Saver, the two most prevalent stereotypes. The Spender believes that they are living a happy life, one that is comfortable, healthy, and enjoyable for the whole family. The Saver uses words like frivolous, careless, impulsive, excessive, or self-indulgent to describe the Spender. The Saver sees themselves as prudent, realistic and smart. The value of money to the saver is achievement, stability, success, power and a lasting legacy. The Spender uses words like mean, frugal, self-centered, cheap, and a hoarder who doesn't know how to appreciate pleasure to describe The Saver. The truth is that we are both the Spender and Saver at different times. The problem that money causes is not about the numbers; it's about what money represents. Money can be used to buy security and pleasure. It is important for couples to strike a balance between the security and trust that money also conveys and the independence and empowerment that it stands for. Each partner enters the relationship with a unique financial background, financial relationship, and feelings related to money. Everybody has a financial legacy—a story about what money has meant to their family.

WORKING HARD FOR THE MONEY
Work takes a lot of our time and also requires commitment just like our relationship does. It is very important that you and your partner discuss your dedication to your job and to earning money. Our time is needed for both our work and our relationship. You don't have to pick between the two to have a successful relationship. You just have to find a way to balance both. Working long hours might cause loneliness in a relationship because there is little time for connection. It will require time, dedication, and long hours if you or your partner is starting a business, but as long as you are open and honest about the

commitment you're making to your career and financial future, you discuss it and come to an agreement with your partner beforehand, it doesn't have to be a deal breaker. We all need to work to survive, unless we are independently wealthy. You have to pay your bills. Work can be a source of financial security as well as personal satisfaction, accomplishment, and even a sense of direction, passion, and purpose in life. They are also very important.

SHARING THE LOAD

This type of discussion about employment and finances was unusual in the 1950s. The man was always the breadwinner who left the house each morning to go to work. He earned the money, he had the authority. The woman usually stayed at home to take care of the household duties, including cooking, cleaning, and watching the kids. However, things are different now. Men and women both work and have children. So depending on the situation; responsibilities are shared or one parent stays at home more while the other works. According to research, both men and women value having a successful marriage more than having a successful career. In every decade, love always comes first. The good news is we don't have to choose between the two. According to research, having a happy marriage increases your chances of having a happy career and vice versa. Unpaid labor is one of the main issues that cause issues in a relationship. Couples have more issues over how the household chore is split up than they do about outside or paid jobs. There is no right or wrong way to split the labor in the 21st century; do whatever works for the two of you. The roles of men and women in the workplace are blending. You will need to decide what is best for your relationship and your life as a team. However, you should know that this will change after you have kids, as you change occupations, and as you collaborate to fulfill each other's ambitions. Work is about so much more than just getting paid, and your perspective on what work and money represent will change throughout the course of your lifetime.

TIME IS MONEY

Finding the correct balance can be challenging because work and having money will have different meanings for you at different points in your life. Depending on the professional decisions each of you makes, the relationship will have both expenses and rewards. Make sure your connection is strong enough to withstand moments when work responsibilities seem to take over both your free time and your relationship. Every marriage should agree on their priorities but every couple is different. You should discuss your personal values and priorities with your partner.

MANAGING TIME

It's common for a partner to complain that the other works too much. To have a great marriage, both partners must invest their time and effort. It is important that both parties have a talk that covers both points of view. We tend to equate our jobs and careers with our identity, our purpose, and our sense of self-worth and it drives us to put in long hours. But working long hours on a regular basis has a cost; you and your partner can start to feel emotionally estranged, which jeopardizes your relationship. Ask each other the following questions if your time together is limited because of one or both of your job schedules;

For the partner working long hours: How important is your work to you? What fulfillment or joy does your work bring you? What need in your life does your job satisfy? If money were no object and you were free from the need to work, how would you spend your day?

For the partner who is frustrated by the long hours: What does the absence of your partner mean to you? What about your partner do you miss while they are gone so much? What kind of connection do you want with your partner? These questions will help you come to an understanding whenever long work hours become a problem in your relationship. Our connection is affected by the way we choose to spend our time. Take some time to consider your typical, 24-hour day.

THE REAL VALUE OF MONEY

Our past financial experiences can have unexpected effects on our relationships. It's important to investigate your family's heritage with regard to riches, charity, influence, and power. What emotional memories and beliefs do you have about poverty, dependence and independence, strength and weakness, philanthropy, civic duty, luxury, and sense of accomplishment? When two people with different financial backgrounds get together, they must overcome the challenge of combining their two histories or face the repercussions of doing nothing about it. The first stage is to become aware of your own past. Understanding your partner's past is the next stage.

HOW MUCH IS ENOUGH?

The term "enough money" means different things to different people. So, how much is enough? Living above their means, entering a relationship with one spouse heavily in debt, concealing financial matters from one another, or failing to collaborate to reach a shared financial goal are all signs that a couple has money issues. Everyone has both short-term and long-term goals. Together, you can create a budget that will help you fulfill both your short- and long-term financial needs and goals. Although you each make up one half of a financial team, your opinion on how much money is enough could be very different. This is because money has different symbolic meanings. Having "enough" money means many different things to women. Women tend to link having "enough" money with having stability, affection, and respect. It is connected with strength, attractiveness, and acceptance. Usually, money and power play a role in men's relationships. Men tend to associate having money with being capable, dependable, and a provider. It is connected with being strong, independent, mature, competitive, powerful, and successful. The fact is that money has significance beyond the costs, the budgets, and the math involved in saving and spending. Discovering your own and your partner's values around money is the goal of this conversation.

LESSONS
1. Balancing your relationship and your work is very important in order to have a successful relationship or marriage.
2. Money issues in a relationship aren't usually about the currency; it is about what money means to each person in a relationship.
3. The two prevalent stereotypes when it comes to money are the Saver and the Spender.
4. Work can be a source of financial, personal satisfaction, accomplishment, and a sense of direction.
5. Our past financial experiences can have unexpected effects on our relationship. This is why we need to have these discussions with your partner so they can understand your perspective.
6. We all have short and long term goals and it is important that we discuss them with our partner.
7. To have a great marriage, both partners must invest their time and effort.
8. Women tend to link having enough money with having stability, affection, and respect while men tend to associate having money with being capable, dependable, and a provider.

QUESTIONS
1. What does money mean to your family?

_____
_____
_____
_____
_____
_____

_____
_____
_____
_____
_____
_____

2. What does your typical day consist of?

_____
_____
_____
_____
_____
_____
_____
_____
_____
_____

3. What does the term "enough money" mean to you?

_____
_____
_____
_____
_____
_____
_____
_____
_____
_____

4. What did your parents teach you about money and how do you currently feel about those teachings?

_____
_____
_____

_____
_____
_____
_____
_____
_____
_____
_____
_____

5. What are your short and long term goals?

_____
_____
_____
_____
_____
_____
_____
_____
_____
_____
_____

6. How's your partner's view of money different from yours?

_____
_____
_____
_____
_____
_____
_____
_____
_____
_____
_____
_____

7. How do you currently feel about work?

_____

_____

_____

_____

_____

_____

_____

_____

_____

_____

_____

8. What is your biggest fear when it comes to money?

_____

_____

_____

_____

_____

_____

_____

_____

_____

_____

_____

_____

_____

9. What is your biggest goal when it comes to work?

_____

_____

_____

_____

_____

_____

10. What compromises have you made when it comes to solving money problems in your relationship?

DATE 5: ROOM TO GROW: FAMILY

OBJECTIVES
1. Defining family.
2. Understanding the marriage curve.
3. The benefits of a loving relationship.

When you don't know how family life will turn out, talking about it can be difficult. Family is the most important thing and it means different things to different people. Nowadays, families are diverse in terms of race, politics, sexual orientation, and religion. Families can include your husband's closest friend or your own biological children. Families with same-sex parents or trans parents are also increasing in number. Family can be summed up as any place or person with whom you feel affection, a sense of belonging, or a sense of home. However you and your partner choose to define family now or in the future is up to you. The most important thing is that you both discuss what family means and what you want your family to be like. If one of you wants kids and the other doesn't, it could mean the end of the relationship. You're setting yourself up for failure if you get married hoping you can persuade or change your partner's mind. It's important to talk about if you want kids and how many kids each of you picture in your dream family.

STAY AHEAD OF THE CURVE
When you welcome a child into your relationship, you feel great love and selflessness. It's impossible to put into words how you fall in love with your child. Falling in love with your partner is one thing, but falling in love with your newborn child for the first time is way better. Children require, demand, and deserve your love, time, and attention, but this shouldn't come at the expense of your relationship with each other. Sociologist Ernest Burgess was one of the first people to investigate married couples. In the 1930s he wanted to build a scientific way to predict the success rates of marriages. In his long-term research of married couples, he discovered that marital pleasure followed a U-shaped curve starting with newlyweds. After the wedding, marital satisfaction started to decline. It then took a significant drop after the first kid was born, and it continued to decline more with each additional child. When the youngest child moved out of the house and the couple didn't get divorced, marital happiness started to rise. If you want to have children and avoid the bottom of the U-shaped curve, there are 2 things to do:

1. Both partners should work to stay involved throughout the pregnancy and birth of children. Both should be involved as equally as possible with the new baby, whether they are same sex or heterosexual couples. In heterosexual couples, studies show that dad's involvement matters greatly, and the secret to keeping dad involved with the child is to make sure that he feels included in all aspects of the pregnancy and child's life.
2. Maintaining your intimacy and connection is the second important factor. You must prioritize your relationship. If you don't divorce first, you will hit the bottom of the curve and won't climb back up for 18 years. You need to make time for connection, talk about your worries with each other, avoid shutting down or withdrawing from each other, and avoid being defensive, critical, or disrespectful in order to maintain intimacy.

SLEEP AND SEX

One of the major concerns about having kids is that it will put an end to your sexual life, leave you with no time for romance, travel, or ambition, and that your marriage and career would suffer as a result. Things like this happen. If you decide to start a family, it is important to continue to set out a special time for your relationship, to have a fulfilling sexual life, and to develop rituals that foster closeness and intimacy. A loving relationship between parents is the best gift for a child. This will serve as the basis for the rest of their lives.

LESSONS
1. Family means different things to different people; it is up to you and your partner to create your own definition.
2. It is important to talk about the kind of family you want with your partner to avoid issues in future.
3. Having children shouldn't be an obstacle to your relationship with your partner, make time for each other.
4. A loving relationship benefits not only the parent but also the children as it serves as a foundation for them.

QUESTIONS
1. What does family mean to you?

_____
_____
_____
_____
_____

_____
_____
_____
_____
_____
_____
_____
_____

2. What concerns do you have or did you have about adding children to your relationship or marriage?

_____
_____
_____
_____
_____
_____
_____
_____
_____
_____

3. How has having a child affected your relationship?

_____
_____
_____
_____
_____
_____
_____
_____
_____
_____
_____
_____
_____
_____

_____
_____
_____
_____
_____
_____
_____
_____

4. What does your ideal family look like?

_____
_____
_____
_____
_____
_____
_____
_____
_____
_____

5. How have your experiences with your family affected your relationships?

_____
_____
_____
_____
_____
_____
_____
_____
_____
_____
_____
_____
_____
_____

6. What problems do you think your relationship might have with maintaining intimacy in your future family?

_____
_____
_____
_____
_____
_____
_____
_____
_____
_____
_____
_____

7. What can be done to avoid the bottom of the U-shaped curve?

_____
_____
_____
_____
_____
_____
_____
_____
_____
_____
_____
_____
_____
_____
_____
_____
_____
_____
_____

DATE 6: PLAY WITH ME: FUN & ADVENTURE

OBJECTIVES
1. Understanding the importance of play in a relationship.
2. Finding common ground.
3. Learning about the brain's reward system.

Play and adventure makes our lives and relationships better, happier, and more enjoyable. Our relationships rely on play in important and necessary ways. It doesn't matter if you and your partner have different opinions of fun and adventure. What matters is finding the time to play together and help each other. Stress, demanding family obligations and long job hours can completely drain the joy out of a relationship. Play is about connecting with one another. Playing with your partner helps build intimacy and trust. Play fosters cooperation in adult relationships in the same way it teaches cooperation to children. Finding ways to play together as often as possible will help your relationship thrive.

LAUGHTER IS THE BEST MEDICINE
Laughter is the emotional foundation of play. Playing can be done while doing the dishes, mowing the lawn etc. Play is spontaneous and all about friendship. There's usually a lot of play at the beginning of a relationship and this doesn't have to end as your relationship becomes serious. In reality, you should work harder and more consistently to make play a part of your daily routines and the fabric of your relationship. All animals have an adventure or seeking system. In humans, it is centered on exploration and curiosity. Humans are highly evolved so we look for new experiences, knowledge and meaning. We also look for the joy and fulfillment that comes with these new experiences. The neuronal network in your brain known as the Reward System is active whenever you experience joy, excitement, or happiness. The neurons of the ventral tegmental, the basal ganglia, the prefrontal cortex, and the nucleus accumbens are all part of this brain circuit. This system also plays a role in learning, motivating ourselves, and finding new and exciting things in life. The main neurotransmitter in the reward system is dopamine. When you get enough of it, you feel happy. The brain gets a dopamine reward whenever you experience something new and different. The problem is when two partners get this brain reward in 2 different ways. According to some scientific studies, some people may have a genetic variation in their dopamine system that makes them seek out riskier behavior and activities. A University of British Columbia researcher named Cynthia Thomson

has discovered what she calls the "Daredevil Gene." For some people, this gene limits the amount of dopamine released and this makes them look for higher and more difficult levels of adventure to get the same reward.

FINDING COMMON GROUND

We all have the natural need to look for new things and be challenged. It doesn't go away even when we're older. Play and adventure for a couple is all about encouraging each other's natural curiosity while also learning, growing, and exploring together. There is a hint of danger in every adventure because it involves the unknown. Your partner's risk tolerance could be different so it is important that you find common ground. This is done by exploring your similarities and differences.

THE CHRISTIE BRINKLEY PHENOMENON

Couples tend to feel a strong sense of bonding after overcoming a struggle or participating in a risky adventure. According to research, there are some similarities between the physiological reactions to arousal and fear. However, you don't have to put your life in danger in order to feel passion in your relationship. The right amygdala, which is connected to the area of the brain responsible for sexual desire, is where we experience fear. When we go on a new or exciting journey, there is also a physiological component at work: a small cocktail of dopamine, norepinephrine, and phenylethylamine (PEA). PEA is the chemical cocktail that causes the intoxicating effect of falling in love. Its levels are also increased by high-intensity activities. Our bodies can build up a tolerance to the effects of PEA and we misinterpreted it as the end of love but it isn't. We can reactivate PEA by recognizing our need for adventure and exploration in our relationships.

ADVENTURING TOGETHER

Our desire to play and have an adventure never goes away. One sign that there isn't enough adventure is when one or both of you start looking for alternatives to the dopamine response and end up feeding the need for play and adventure with junk food, alcohol, drugs, etc. Relationships with no shared adventure or no adventure of any kind become boring and turn to a task. Adventures don't need to be expensive or put you in serious danger. You and your partner don't have to play in the same ways to be a happy couple. However, you still need adventure. It is important that you talk about how your play makes you feel while showing them images and stories. Look at the world with new eyes and curiosity. When it comes to play and adventure, you can have different interests and still have a healthy, thriving relationship. However, look for the places where your play and adventure intersect. A relationship without play is a relationship without laughter, flirting, games, or fantasy. We all need laughter, play, and humor; it should be a priority. Don't make the mistake of assuming that you will play together once all the work is over. It won't happen.

LESSONS
1. Playing with your partner builds trust, intimacy and connection.
2. It's not a bad thing if you and your partner have different meanings of play and adventure.
3. A relationship without play is a relationship without laughter, flirting, games, or fantasy.
4. The right amygdala is where we experience fear and sexual arousal.
5. We have an adventure seeking system and it is centered on curiosity and exploration.
6. Our reward system becomes active whenever we experience joy, excitement, or happiness.
7. Dopamine is the main neurotransmitter in our reward system and we are happy when we get enough of it.
8. Our desire to play never goes away even as we get older.

QUESTIONS
1. What are the advantages of adventure and play in a relationship?

_____
_____
_____
_____
_____
_____
_____
_____
_____
_____
_____
_____
_____
_____
_____
_____
_____

2. What does adventure mean to you?

_____

_____

_____

_____

_____

_____

_____

_____

_____

_____

_____

_____

3. What's your partner's idea of play and adventure?

_____

_____

_____

_____

_____

_____

_____

_____

_____

_____

_____

4. What's the most fun you've had with your partner recently?

_____

_____

_____

_____

_____

_____

_____

_____

_____

5. What are the similarities in the way you and your partner like to have fun?

_____

_____

_____

_____

_____

_____

_____

_____

_____

_____

6. What are the differences in the way you and your partner like to have fun?

_____

_____

_____

_____

_____

_____

_____

_____

_____

_____

7. What adventure would you like to have with your partner?

_____

_____

_____

_____

_____

_____

_____

_____

_____

_____

_____

8. What are your replacements for play when you need a dopamine rush?

_____

_____

_____

_____

_____

_____

_____

_____

_____

_____

9. What is the function of the PEA?

_____

_____

_____

_____

_____

_____

_____

_____

_____

_____

_____

10. How do you think you can you have more fun in your relationship?

_____

_____

_____

_____

DATE 7: SOMETHING TO BELIEVE IN: GROWTH & SPIRITUALITY

OBJECTIVES
1. Creating meaning.
2. Accommodating growth and change.

Amazing things happen in relationships when a couple is willing to adapt to each other's growth and progress. Relationships can be more than just two people getting along; they can be stories of transformation, contribution and meaning in the world.

CREATING SHARED MEANING
Change is the one constant in relationships and life. The important thing is how each partner in the relationship accommodates the other's growth. People develop in relationships because they interact with minds different from their own. However, any form of change, even spiritual change can cause issues in relationships. Remember, conflict is necessary for a relationship to grow, so it is important that we embrace it as a method to improve our love for one another. Life and relationships can be difficult. According to research on married couples, a couple will have a better relationship if they treat their union as sacred. Your relationship will be deeper, richer, and more fulfilling if you can find more shared meaning to create together. So how do you give your relationship meaning? How do you treat your bond with respect? We do this by creating shared meaning and personal rituals for connection. The rituals you build together will help make your relationship stronger. Think about how you can celebrate small and big wins in life. Think about how you can create routines to deal with loss, setbacks, bad luck, and exhaustion. There are different ways to create meaning with your partner. It could be talking about your day. You have the chance to respect all that is precious in your relationship at every opportunity.

GROWING AND CHANGING
Making it comfortable for your spouse to share the strange and showing genuine curiosity about the growth they're going through are two ways to accommodate growth and change in a relationship. Relationships develop as people do. Relationships change when people change. Making it safe for your partner to talk about strange things and showing genuine curiosity about their development are two ways to accommodate growth and change in a relationship. Relationships grow when people mature. Relationships also change as people do.

LESSONS
1. Change is a constant in our lives and relationships.
2. Relationships grow as people mature and change.
3. Rituals with your partner help relationships to become stronger and better.
4. Finding more shared meaning with your partner helps your relationship be deeper and more fulfilling.
5. You give your relationship meaning by creating shared meaning and personal rituals for connection.

QUESTIONS
1. What do you consider sacred in your relationship?

_____
_____
_____
_____
_____
_____
_____
_____
_____
_____
_____
_____

2. What rituals do you have with your partner?

_____
_____
_____
_____
_____
_____
_____
_____
_____
_____
_____
_____
_____

3. How has your relationship helped you grow?

_____

_____

_____

_____

_____

_____

_____

_____

_____

_____

_____

4. How has your partner changed and grown since your relationship started?

_____

_____

_____

_____

_____

_____

_____

_____

_____

_____

_____

5. What routines do you have to deal with negative situations?

_____

_____

_____

_____

_____

_____

_____

_____

_____

6. How have you accommodated your partner's growth and change?

_____

_____

_____

_____

_____

_____

_____

_____

_____

_____

_____

7. What are the benefits of creating shared meaning?

_____

_____

_____

_____

_____

_____

_____

_____

_____

_____

_____

8. How has your relationship changed as you and your partner grew?

_____

_____

_____

_____

_____

_____

DATE 8: A LIFETIME OF LOVE: DREAMS

OBJECTIVES
1. Understanding the importance of dreams.
2. Working with your partner.
3. Knowing how to make compromises.

Work takes a lot of time and energy especially if you're struggling to make ends meet, pay off college loans etc. We already have a commitment to our partners and employers, and making a promise to pursue a goal may seem like more responsibility to manage. Dreams are very important; your dreams, your spouse's dream etc. Dreaming with your partner and encouraging one another to pursue individual goals are equally important to your partnership as commitment, sex, and trust. One of the most meaningful things you can do in a relationship is to dream together. Honoring your partner's dreams is also a powerful way to show someone you care about them. Everything else in a relationship becomes easier because each person feels supported to follow their dreams. Everyone has a life goal or ambition, and it is very important that you don't give up on your goals or dreams in favor of your job, your family, or even your relationship.

TAKING TURNS
While everyone makes compromises, you cannot give up on your dreams. They cannot be repressed. This can cause a great deal of distance in a relationship as well as bitterness, resentment, and a loss of passion and desire. As partners, we must support one another in finding a method to channel and follow our aspirations, whether they be for work or for leisure. This maintains the partnership and each partner's passion, vitality, and vigor alive. A companion who is just partially alive is also undesirable. The objective is to maintain your dream while being in a relationship. Go after your goals. And tell your companion about your dreams. You can't give up on your dreams or suppress them. This can cause distance in a relationship by fostering resentment, bitterness, and a loss of passion. It is important that you and your partner work together to pursue each other's dreams. This allows your relationship to remain passionate, energetic, and alive. However, no one wants a partner who is only partially alive. The goal is to be in a relationship while holding on to your goals. Follow your dreams and talk to your partner about your dreams.

BECOME A DREAM TEAM

Your partner has dreams you don't know about and the truth is most of our dreams have their roots in our childhood. Your dreams with your partner are called deep dreams. The most important and significant lesson to learn from dreams is to not keep them secret. It is important that you tell your partner if you want to build something significant. When we hide our dreams, we hide the most important parts of who we are. A dream is something you long and wish for, and if you don't share it with your partner, it can lead to conflict. Ignoring your dream doesn't make it go away. Being upfront and honest about all of your goals is the way to prevent conflict. It is also important to respect and honor your partner's dream even if they are different from your own. Every dream you have and every dream your spouse has is a story. Share your stories with one another, dream together, think together and you can achieve any dream that seems impossible. Our dreams are where we find our greatest joy and learn about the special talents we have to offer the world.

LESSONS
1. A dream is something you long and wish for.
2. We all have dreams and we should try our possible best to fulfill them.
3. Honoring your partner's dreams is also a powerful way to show you care about them.
4. Making compromises is important but it doesn't mean we should give up on our goals.
5. Repressing your dreams can have a negative effect on your relationship; it can cause distance and resentment.
6. When we hide our dreams, we hide the most important parts of ourselves and who we are.

QUESTIONS
1. What dreams did you have as a child?

_____
_____
_____
_____
_____
_____
_____
_____
_____

_____
_____
_____

2. What are your current dreams?

_____
_____
_____
_____
_____
_____
_____
_____
_____
_____
_____

3. What dreams do you and your partner currently have together?

_____
_____
_____
_____
_____
_____
_____
_____
_____
_____
_____

4. What compromises have your partner made to help you achieve a dream?

_____
_____
_____
_____
_____

_____

_____

_____

_____

_____

_____

5. What is your biggest and most important dream?

_____

_____

_____

_____

_____

_____

_____

_____

_____

_____

_____

_____

_____

6. What can you do to help your partner achieve their dreams?

_____

_____

_____

_____

_____

_____

_____

_____

_____

_____

_____

_____

_____

7. What dreams have you given up on and why?

_____

_____

_____

_____

_____

_____

_____

_____

_____

_____

_____

_____

8. How has giving up on a certain dream affected your relationship?

_____

_____

_____

_____

_____

_____

_____

_____

_____

_____

_____

_____

_____

_____

_____

_____

_____

_____

_____

_____

_____

Made in United States
Troutdale, OR
11/18/2023